TEACHING

Excellence
or Survival?

*A Reflective Guide to the Greatest
Profession in the World*

Chuck Benigno, PhD

Teaching: Excellence or Survival?

Published by Wheatmark™
610 East Delano Street, Suite 104, Tucson, Arizona 85705 U.S.A.
www.wheatmark.com

International Standard Book Number: 1-58736-657-6
Library of Congress Control Number: 2006926555

Chuck Benigno
P.O. Box 1166
Laurel, MS, 39441
chuckbenigno@aol.com
(601) 580-1810

DEDICATION

THIS BOOK IS dedicated to the teachers, administrators, school secretaries, bus drivers, janitors, and other school personnel who get up every morning to take care of the children in their community. A special thank you to the students, faculties, and staffs of

St. Paul's High School, Covington, Louisiana
North Forrest High School, Hattiesburg, Mississippi
Bay St. Louis–Waveland School District
West Jones High School, Laurel, Mississippi

Your dedication and love for children has inspired me to share our story of how schools can be "special places to work and learn." It was a privilege to work with you and to learn from you.

On a special note, I want to thank my loving wife Gina and our wonderful children, Kristen, Kaitlin and Brett for allowing me to follow my dreams. Of all the achievements, being husband and father to you is my greatest joy. I love you!

CONTENTS

Lagniappe

INTRODUCTION

FOR MORE THAN twenty years, I have had the privilege of waking up each morning and looking forward to going to work. Sometimes it was because of the topic we were discussing that day. Sometimes it was the big game coming up that night. Sometimes it was the realization that it was the last day before a much needed holiday break. But, no matter what, I have always loved being an educator.

For educators, the annual 180-day journey known as teaching is one of the most fulfilling, demanding, exhausting, exciting, and scariest endeavors ever embarked on. These collections of emotions make us who we are and shape us both personally and professionally.

There is no question that all educators go through stages of just surviving. The key is to not stay in "survival mode." Our students need us to not just *survive* our time with them, but to serve them with and help them to achieve *excellence* in everything they do.

Like no other profession in the world, teaching gives us a chance to make a positive impact on the lives of young people. *Teaching: Excellence or Survival?* is a reflective guide to enjoying and embracing one of the most important and challenging jobs in America.

We truly are "saving lives" every day. Thanks for being a teacher!

1

STRIVE FOR EXCELLENCE

"Good is the enemy of Great."

—JIM COLLINS

I WAS FIRST confused by Jim Collins' quote from his best selling book *Good to Great*. How can good be the enemy of great? Then it hit me. We too often settle for being good. Good is good. However, this mindset stops us from reaching "true excellence" in both our personal and professional lives. If we strive for excellence and miss, we end up being pretty darn good. However, if we strive to be good and miss, we end up being pretty average. Our students deserve better than average. They need us at our best.

Striving for excellence begins with a commitment to do the little extra things that separate average work from quality work. The Greek philosopher Aristotle put it this way: "We are what we repeatedly do. Excellence, then, is not an act, but a habit." The goal is not to just have singular acts of excellence, but to make a habit of pursuing a standard of excellence that becomes part of your reputation. Successful teaching requires developing an aura that permeates the room. Please remember that students, parents, and colleagues are constantly evaluating this atmosphere.

I challenge you to leave no stone unturned in your effort to be the very best teacher that you can be. Go to workshops, visit other teachers' classrooms, videotape yourself. Don't be scared to create a special place for your students to work and learn. Listen to the kids and be there for them. Give them your best, and you can sleep soundly knowing that you are making a difference in your community.

Most importantly, take care of yourself so that you can have the energy and confidence to "fight the good fight." The kids need you now more than ever.

2

GROW OR DIE?

"Growth is the only evidence of life."

—HENRY NEUMAN

HENRY NEUMAN WROTE, "Growth is the only evidence of life." Now I don't know if Mr. Neuman is biologically correct or not; however, I do believe that we either get better or we get worse. We don't stay the same. We either continue to grow as educators, or we begin the downhill slide toward death. You see, it is not about what type of teacher you are now, it is what type of teacher you are going to be three years from now, ten years from now.

When I became principal in 1994, I happened to run across one of my files from my first job as a biology teacher in 1985. As I opened the folder I was embarrassed by what I found. There was my first Chapter 17 test, twenty questions (true-false and matching) written in my ugly printed handwriting. The level of assessment was minimal at best. The only thing that made me feel better and not a total hypocrite was what I found in the back of the same folder. It was my Chapter 17 test after my fifth year of teaching biology. It was forty questions, typed neatly (before computers) with three truly engaging discussion questions. To this day, it seemed like a really challenging test. It was the perfect example of the evolution of teaching.

You see, in that first year I really thought I was a good

teacher; however, in hindsight, I was probably not. After five years of growth and development, I was slowly becoming a pretty good teacher. This is my challenge to you. Never stop growing and striving to become an expert in your field. You will be energized by the journey and most importantly, your students will benefit from their access to a true master teacher.

3

IN THE BATTLE

It is not the critic who counts, not the man who points out how the strong man stumbled, or where the doer of deeds could have done better. The credit belongs to the man (woman) who is actually in the arena, whose face is marred by dust and sweat and blood, who strives valiantly, who errs and comes up short again and again, who knows the great enthusiasms, the great devotions, and spends himself in a worthy cause, who at best knows achievement and who at the worst if he fails at least fails while daring greatly so that his place shall never be with those timid souls who know neither victory or defeat.

—THEODORE ROOSEVELT

THANK YOU FOR being in the arena! Even though there are those who like to criticize and judge the performance of our schools, at least we are in the battle. It is easy for those on the sideline to take potshots at the ones who are actually in the arena. I don't know about you, but I don't see a whole lot of people lined up for our jobs. Nevertheless, we cannot let this lack of job competitiveness lead us to complacency. Our children deserve to have us at our best.

President Roosevelt's words capture the essence of being a teacher. Doing it right requires blood, sweat and dusting off your pants as you pick yourself off the arena floor. Oh, but the joy of great enthusiasms, such as the hug of a child, beginning readers, touchdown passes, earned scholarships, and handwritten thank you notes! Teaching is a worthy cause, and no one knows better than the teacher about the triumphs and failures of this noble mission.

So, let us continue to dare greatly, so to never be mentioned with the timid souls who have never invested in the lives of young people.

4

THE BEST TEACHING

"The best teaching is not in front of the classroom, but in between the aisles and over the shoulders of students."

—CHUCK BENIGNO

I WAS GIVING a presentation on classroom management to a neighboring school district when it hit me like a bolt of lightening. We were reflecting on the keys to an effective classroom. I was doing my spill on the importance of teacher movement around the room when I realized what good teaching was and where it occurred. It has led me to this simple, yet powerful summary:

"The best teaching is not in front of the classroom, but in between the aisles and over the shoulders of students."

This philosophy comes to light every time I walk through a math classroom while students are doing a seated assignment. In a matter of three minutes, I can walk around the room and figure out who is lost, who has mastered the material, and who hasn't even started. I then begin the process of leaning over the shoulders of students who need help. There is the key!

Even when we are doing our best "song and dance" in front of the class, many of our students are zoned out. Too many teachers follow this introductory lesson with a class assignment and then proceed to sit at their desk to grade papers or conduct other teacher tasks. These teachers are missing the most teachable moment of the day.

If we want quality work from our students, we must be willing to work the room. We cannot afford to wait until next Friday's chapter test to realize that Johnny and Susie are totally lost.

The diversity of the 21st century classroom and the demands of high-stakes testing require us to take advantage of every instructional moment. Please add over the shoulder, pulled-up desk instruction to your daily repertoire. This is where you might see a student's light come on or hear the most magical words spoken by a student, "Oh, I get it."

5

REMEMBER WHAT IT'S LIKE TO BE A KID

"Everybody gets so much information all day long that they lose their common sense."

—GERTRUDE STEIN (1874–1946)

THE BEST TEACHERS are those who can remember what it was like to be a kid. The ability to look through the lens of the other person is what separates those who can touch the heart of another. Don't you remember that first day of school wanting your hair and clothes to be just right? What about Billy who just got a note in the hallway from his girlfriend telling him she wanted to break up? The bell rings and here he comes to class and you want him to focus on photosynthesis? To Billy, the world is over.

Being cognizant of the importance of pep rallies, proms, field trips to the pumpkin patch, and other activities that make up the school culture is essential for the difference-making educator. Today's kids face a different type of world. If Gertrude Stein thought the information overload of the 1940's was enough to cause one to lose common sense, then she would really understand why common sense rarely raises its beautiful head in the year 2006.

Today's kids are experiencing what I call the two-three year curve. A fifteen-year-old today is dealing with issues that you and I didn't have to deal with until we were seventeen or eighteen. The problem is that they are no more physically, emotionally, or spiritually ready to handle these issues than we would have been at fifteen years old. It is not the kids' fault; it is society's fault, and we must take these issues into consideration when trying to figure out why they do what they do.

The examples listed below are stark reminders of the different influences shaping students' lives. Here is a look at my after-school experience compared to today's kids.

Yesterday (1970's)	**Today (2006)**
Mom is home	Mom is at work
3 channels (NBC, ABC, CBS)	152 channels
Shows: Gilligan's Island, Brady Bunch	Jerry Springer, Punked
Sexiest Decision: Ginger or Mary Ann	MTV or Victoria Secret's Special
Activity: Played ball until dark	Play video games inside

6

JOURNEY TOGETHER

"It is good to have an end to journey toward, but it is the journey that matters in the end."

—URSULA K. LEGUIN

THE 180-DAY SCHOOL year is a journey through time that must not be wasted. Teaching presents a wonderful opportunity to develop relationships with young people. If you truly want a relationship with your students, you must be willing to let them know who you are as a person. Even though we must be careful not to cross the line by becoming too personal or being unprofessional, it is important that students know our qualifications (degree, teaching resume', professional organizations, etc.) and other pertinent information that can contribute to our credibility. As you introduce yourself, you begin to break down the walls that many times keep us from truly reaching students.

The great artist attempts to make a connection with his/her audience. My wife and I went to see Martina McBride in concert. We were fortunate to see her in a relatively small and intimate auditorium, and throughout the evening she shared stories about her life. While she sang different songs, pictures of her family were being shown on the video screen. These images made us feel like we really knew who she was. Later, she shared that she was from Kansas and that watching the *Wizard of Oz* for her family was a huge annual TV event. She then proceeded to sing "Somewhere Over the Rainbow" and it put chills up our spine. She had us, and we loved her.

Throughout my teaching career, it was natural for me to share tidbits about my life in an effort to make a connection with my students. During the flow of the year, there would always be an appropriate time for me to share my family's journey to America. I would share that my great grandfather came from Italy in the early 1900's and could not speak a word of English. He became a farmer and delivered vegetables and fresh bread on a horse and buggy all around the coastal towns of Bay St. Louis and Pass Christian, Mississippi. He was really doing well until 1929 when he lost his little farm in the Great Depression. His son, my grandfather, was a shrimper who for forty years would leave the Pass Christian harbor on a boat named the *Jo Ann* and head into the Gulf of Mexico in search for shrimp. His son, my dad, worked for the power company and had a couple of years of college education. I went on to become a teacher and was the first of these four gentlemen to have a college degree. These insights helped my students to see me as a person.

During the course of a typical year, you and your students will experience events ranging from birth to death and just about every other emotion in between. This emotional journey can benefit you and the students. Together, you can be a source of strength and comfort for one another. Enjoy the ride!

7

THE MOST IMPORTANT DAY

"Children are like wet cement. Whatever falls on them makes an impression."

—HIAM GINOTT

OVER THE PAST several years, I have had the privilege of speaking to numerous schools and have personally implemented in three different school districts the principles outlined by Dr. Harry Wong and his book *The First Days of School*. This book is a must read for every educator. Dr. Wong emphasizes a number of areas that lead to teacher effectiveness and highlights the procedures that can help you start your year off on a positive note.

The unlimited potential and magical nature of starting each school year with a clean slate allows the teacher to dream of the perfect year. If you want a journey of excellence and not just survival, then you must understand the importance of the first day of school. I don't care what you have to do; make sure you have your room ready and inviting for this first day. By being organized and prepared, you can relax enough to greet your students and not be distracted by last minute details that stop you from making a personal contact with your students.

Another strategy that Dr. Wong advocates, and one that I have required in all of our schools, is that students have assigned seats waiting for them when they walk into the classroom for the first time. I have seen it done several ways; however our teachers have been most successful by having each desk numbered in their room. As they greet and introduce themselves to each student at the door, they simply look at the roll and tell them what number they have. I believe this extra step shows the student that we are organized and in charge of the class.

Remember, first impressions are powerful. You can't get back that first opportunity to introduce yourself and the expectations you have for the upcoming school year. It is during this first impression that many of your students will make judgments about you and your class. In the first thirty seconds of your introduction the students are determining if this is a place they want to be. Their little minds are asking: Is the teacher going to be boring or exciting, will I be treated with respect, and does this person know what he or she is talking about? This is why it is imperative that the teacher conducts this day in a way that clearly states that they are organized, professional, knowledgeable, and caring.

8

TEACH PROCEDURES

"The number one problem in the classroom is not discipline; it is the lack of procedures and routines."

—DR. HARRY WONG

THE REASON WHY the first days of school are so important is that during this narrow window of opportunity, students will for the most part do what we tell them to do. If we get in too big of a hurry to introduce subject matter and don't take the time to explain how we expect students to perform everyday procedures, we will find ourselves playing cops and robbers for the rest of the year.

Don't assume that students know what we expect of them. The effective teacher uses the first few weeks to explain, rehearse, and reinforce the procedures for classroom activities. Once these positive habits are formed, learning can take place. Dr. Wong states it clearly, "It is the procedures that set the class up for success." The following is a list of just a few of the procedures that should be taught:

Entering the classroom	Class dismissal
Use of restroom	Asking questions
Turning in papers	Quieting the class
Sharpening pencils	Working in groups

P.S. Without a doubt, the #1 procedure that is a must for effective classroom management is the use of pre-bell (bellwork) activities to ensure that students get to work immediately. A Google search on the web will introduce you to lots of good ideas for quality bellwork. One web site is www.bellwork.com. Examples of quality pre-bell assignments include:

"Quote of the Day" Reflections
Newspaper Articles
Daily Oral Language Activities
Math Problems
Sample State Test Questions
Journal Entries
Brain Teasers
Dictionary Searches

Grading Bellwork: For bellwork to be effective, students must know that they will be held accountable for this daily activity. However, teachers have enough on their plate and do not have the time to grade bellwork everyday. Remember, the grade should be determined by whether the student followed the procedure more than whether the answer was correct or not. The following guidelines are suggested to streamline the bellwork process:

1. Each Monday, have the students create or you can supply a bellwork sheet that has space noted for Monday-Friday.

2. Check bellwork every Friday for a grade.

3. Keep it simple: Take a quick glance and if the student has all five days of assignments then they get a 100. If they go 4 for 5 they get an 80. This continues with a possibility of the student receiving a zero.

4. If the student is absent from class just have them put the word "absent" in the space for that day. Do not try to coordinate make-up bellwork.

9

HOW TO START CLASS

"This one step—choosing a goal and sticking to it— changes everything."

—SCOTT REED

THIS TOPIC COULD just as well be titled "How not to start a class." Too many teachers are starting class with words like "Everyone sit down, It's time to get started, or Quiet please." Then, when they finally get every one's attention, they begin the ineffective process of calling out names to find out who is present and who is not. After six or seven periods of starting class this way, the teacher is miserable and everyone pays the price for his or her disposition.

A huge part of Dr. Harry Wong's philosophy on effective classroom management can be found in the use of pre-bell assignments (bellwork). It is imperative that students immediately get to work as soon as they enter the classroom. The effective teacher has a short three to five minute assignment already on the board waiting on the students, and the assignment is always in the same location every day.

The key to successful implementation of this procedure is what I call "Zip and Walk." When the bell rings to start class, if we will simply say "Good Morning!" and zip our mouths as we begin to walk between the aisles, students will get to work and be quiet. However, so often, we as teachers break the silence by asking or accepting questions. During this three to five minute period, speak only in a whisper as you walk between the aisles. Then, when you have the class where you want it, tiptoe over and check roll.

Please note that zipping without walking is a recipe for failure. It is the initial walking between the aisles that assures student participation and increased quality of work.

Perfect example: We had blocked off one half of the hallway to administer the state test to all algebra students. As the bell rang, students at the other end of the hall began to exchange classes. I noticed that one teacher had a laminated newspaper article already on each desk for the incoming students. His procedure was for the students to read the article and write a short summary for bellwork. I was impressed by his organization, and as the tardy bell rang to begin class, I moved back toward the testing area. It was at this time that I heard a commotion in the class across the hall. It hit me like a bolt of lightning. The teacher didn't have a pre-bell. I had to find out if my instincts were correct. Sure enough, I stuck my head in the door of the noisy, unorganized room and I saw no bellwork. I decided to check on the gentleman who had his articles already on the desk. There he was, enjoying the wonderful world of teaching. His kids were working, and he was walking around quietly checking roll. In the other room, no one was working, the teacher was miserable, and in her opinion, the kids were terrible. Who is really the problem?

Embrace the silence. Simply say "Good Morning" and then "Zip and Walk."

10

PASSION

*"The road to happiness lies in two simple principles;
find what interests you and that you can do well, and
put your whole soul into it - every bit of energy and
ambition and natural ability you have."*

—JOHN D. ROCKEFELLER

IF YOU WANT to be successful, you have to be passionate
about what you are doing. It should be evident to anyone
who comes in contact with you that you love what you are
doing and believe in its importance. You must live, eat, and
breathe your teaching. Now, I don't mean that you don't
find time for the other aspects of your life. What I do mean
is that you are alert at all times for information or ideas
that can be added to your repertoire. You are constantly
striving to learn more about your area of expertise.

Some of my greatest ideas have come at seventy-five
mph on Interstate 59 between Hattiesburg and Laurel,
Mississippi. Now, I don't advocate writing while you're
driving. However, when the inspiration hits you, you better do something with it. I can't tell you how many times
I have written something down on a napkin in a restau-
rant or gotten out of bed to write a good idea down. Having things that get me out of bed at 1:30 in the morning
is what makes me feel alive. Leadership expert, Dr. John
Maxwell, states it clearly, "There is no substitute for pas-

sion. It is the fuel for the will. If you want anything badly enough, you can find the willpower to achieve it."

If you want students to care about your subject, then they must feel your enthusiasm for the material. They need to hear that this idea came to you at seventy-five mph on I-59 or at 1:30 in the morning. If they don't see passion, then how can you expect them to become engaged? Whether it is world history, literature, biology, music or art, make sure your classroom is filled with the infectious disease called passion.

11

ENERGY

"Success in almost any field depends more on energy and drive than it does on intelligence."

—SLOAN WILSON

WHAT BETTER ROLE model for a teacher than the "Energizer Bunny"! It just keeps going and going and going! The best teachers possess this same boundless energy. All of us have different personalities. However, those teachers who are constantly moving around the room are much better able to manage and motivate young people. You need to be able to "sing and dance" if you want to reach today's kids. I wish they could sit quietly while we lecture all day, but they can't. They live in a fast paced, text messaging, microwave world that requires us to hustle for their attention.

Moving around the room is not the only benefit of high energy. With high energy levels, you can embrace the many unique challenges that each school day presents. Whether it is the surprise principal evaluation, the crying child, or the jammed copy machine, an energized person has a chance to turn it up a notch when necessary. When you're tired, your students suffer. Take a look at your diet and sleep habits. Start exercising today. Show me someone who exercises regularly, and I'll show you someone who has an extra bounce in his/her step. All aspects of your life will be invigorated by a healthier, more energetic you.

KEY TO SUCCESS

The best advice for teachers is not
"Don't smile until Christmas"

The best advice is
"Don't sit until Labor Day"

12

HUMOR

"Laughter is the shortest distance between two people."

—Victor Borge

LET'S BE HONEST. In this crazy business called education, if we don't do some laughing we are going to do a lot of crying. Of course we should never laugh at the expense of others. However, the school setting is capable of creating some really funny occasions. Having a sense of humor is a prerequisite for anyone to survive the day-to-day challenges of being a teacher. First and foremost, we need to be able to laugh at ourselves. Don't take yourself so seriously. Secondly, there is considerable research stating that laughter is good for the soul and your health.

I recently got a chuckle when I walked into the seventh grade boys' bathroom and heard the sound of several boys horse playing. As they all scattered toward the different stalls, there was Thomas, still wearing his gloves from the cold morning with his hands under the running water of the sink. I said, "Thomas, if you are going to wash your hands, you might want to take off your gloves." We all laughed, and I told them to get their tails to class.

Whether it is your interaction with the class clown or the time you tripped over a book bag in front of the class, use humor as a way to develop a relationship with your class. Working with young people can cause numerous health conditions. In many cases, "Laughter is the best medicine."

13

RESPECT

"Every person is entitled to be valued by their best moments."

—RALPH WALDO EMERSON

As ARETHA FRANKLIN sings so passionately "All I'm asking for is a little respect", she captures a most human need, the need to be respected. As educators, we are constantly striving to have others respect us. We have a particular desire for our students to respect us. I have come to believe that the only way for one to get respect is to give respect. I think it is especially true when it comes to our relationship with our students. We must create an atmosphere in which everyone in the class feels that he/she is valued and treated with dignity. How do we create such an environment? It all begins with the way we talk to one another.

When talking to new members of our staff, I always begin by sharing our school philosophy. In this discussion, I create a scenario that exemplifies how I want our students treated. If the teacher says, " Hey boy, come here," and the student replies "Who you calling boy?" right away we have a confrontation. Now, I'm going to support the teacher because I'm not going to allow a student to argue with an adult. However, the teacher's tone of voice and choice of words contributed to the problem. The key is to not give the students any ammunition. By addressing students respectfully and refusing to get down on their level in times of conflict, we maintain a level of professionalism that earns the students' respect.

The key to becoming a difference-making educator lies in the desire and ability to create a relationship with the students who are entrusted to our care. In your very first address to the students, it is important that they hear that you are excited to be there, that you will treat them with dignity and respect, and that you expect the same from them. As the year progresses, there will be times when you will need to privately address certain students who are not showing you the proper respect. The greatest tool you possess is the ability to say without hesitation, "Haven't I always treated you with respect?" and the student knows you are telling the truth.

Respect is a two way street. As the adults, it is our responsibility to go first.

14

HARD WORK

The heights by great men reached and kept
Were not obtained by sudden flight,
But they, while their companions slept,
Were toiling upward in the night

—HENRY WADSWORTH LONGFELLOW

THERE IS NO substitute for hard work. If you want to be successful, you must be willing to pay the price. One of my favorite books is Rick Pitino's *Success is a Choice*. In this book he makes reference to "Deserving Victory." In his introduction Coach Pitino states: "You want to succeed? Okay, then succeed. Deserve it. How? Outwork everybody in sight. Sweat the small stuff. Sweat the big stuff. Go the extra mile. But whatever it takes, put your heart and soul into everything you do."

In education, paying the price often includes long hours, low pay, and lack of appreciation. The successful teacher reduces the hours through organization, increases the salary through higher qualifications, and earns appreciation through the development of relationships.

The first step to becoming an outstanding educator is to work harder than everyone else. Many educators have a negative opinion of coaches. Some of the best academic teachers I know have also been coaches. Unfortunately, some coaches only use their passion and energy on the field and not in the classroom. However, we can learn a great deal from the effort and intensity that coaches put into their sport. We must bring that same energy, enthusiasm, and work ethic into our classrooms. Your subject area is your sport. Strive to win every day.

Bobby Knight once said, "The will to prepare to win is more important than the will to win." Everyone loves to win. The question is, are we willing to put in the preparation necessary for victory?

15

LET'S BE HONKERS

"You can complain because roses have thorns, or you can rejoice because thorns have roses."

—TOM WILSON

WE ALL KNOW them. They whine and complain about everything. Never a positive comment. They would rather die than say something nice about a student, fellow teacher, or the school. How or why did they get into education? Well, that is a story for another day. However, let's talk about how to avoid falling into this same pattern. First and foremost, stay away from these type of people. They are like poison. I know it may sound too simplistic, but if you would just follow an old cliché, life would be so much sweeter. I remember it from the Walt Disney classic *Bambi*. The adorable character Thumper has just made fun of Bambi, and Thumper's mom asks him what his father had told him that morning. Thumper replies, "If you can't say something nice, don't say nothing at all."

They say for every negative comment it takes twelve positive comments to wipe out the negative. Scientists who study geese have determined that they fly in the "V" formation for several specific reasons. One is the benefit of the "honking." By honking, the geese motivate the others to keep up their speed. The problem in education is that the people who are doing most of the "honking" are the negative people. I want you and I to be "honkers." This year, we are going to "honk" so loud that we are going to drown out the negative voices that are killing the spirit of our schools.

It is hard enough to be a young person, teacher, or school. Let's make sure that we are beacons of positive messages. The school culture needs more people who see their glasses half full rather than half empty. If we want our students to have positive attitudes, let us lead by example.

16

THEY NEED TO BE CHALLENGED

"Our greatest glory is not in never falling, but in rising every time we fall."

—CONFUCIUS

I DON'T KNOW about you, but I am tired of feeling like I have to apologize for asking kids to do some work. Except for rare situations, mom and dad are paying the bills and the students number one job should be schoolwork. However, it is our responsibility to make sure that the assignments we require are well thought out, relative to the goals and objectives of the curriculum, and not just the same old worksheets and lecture. That said, we should not apologize for challenging our students.

One of my favorite stories about the consequences of doing too much for children involves the story of the little boy who found a cocoon of a developing butterfly. He put it in a glass mason jar and punched several holes in the top of the lid. After several days of waiting for the butterfly to appear, the little boy's curiosity got the best of him and he decided to take his pocketknife and make a small cut into the cocoon. Sure enough, the butterfly emerged but fell to the bottom of the jar and was unable to fly.

What the boy didn't realize is that it is through the process of busting out of the cocoon that the butterfly develops enough strength to fly. And so it is with our kids. If we don't require them to do some work on their own, we are handicapping them for the upcoming challenges of the real world. The passage below needs to be our new mantra:

The Teacher said to the Students
"Come to the edge"
They replied: "We might fall."
The teacher again said:
"Come to the edge"
and they responded: "It's too high"
"Come to the edge"
the teacher demanded.
And they came
and the teacher pushed them
and they Flew

—GUILLAUME APOLLINAIRE

17

TEAMWORK

Together
Everyone
Achieves
More

TEACHERS SPEND A tremendous amount of time in their
own rooms and in many cases isolated from the other professionals in the building. However, it is important to be
able to work well with others. Whether it is committee
assignments, departmental relationships, or the implementation of school policies, an effective school is one in
which everyone is on the same page. Do not fool yourself
into thinking that you can act within your own little vacu-
um. What you do affects the whole organization. We need
to work together to create a successful learning environment. Remember, there is no "I" in team.

I love the following story shared by Robert Reich, the
former Secretary of Labor during President Clinton's ad-
ministration:

"I call it the pronoun test," says Reich. "I ask front-line
workers a few general questions about the company. If
the answers I get back describe the company in terms like
'they or them', I know it is one kind of company. If the
answers are put in terms like 'we or us' I know it is a different kind of company."

What kind of school is yours? Is it a 'they and them'

or a 'we and us' school? Are we always blaming someone else (the elementary teachers, parents, administrators, too much TV, etc.), or are we willing to take the hand that is dealt to us and make the best of it? It all starts with you!

TEAMWORK LESSON

(author unknown)

WE CAN LEARN a lot from geese on why it is important to work like a team for the betterment of the group.

Did you ever wonder why geese fly in a "V" formation? As each bird flaps its wings, it creates an uplift for the bird in front.

Whenever a goose falls out of formation, it suddenly feels a drag of resistance because it no longer benefits from the one in front.

Teamwork Lesson:
Every member's effort is important.

When the lead goose gets tired, he rotates back in the wing and another goose flies point.

Teamwork Lesson:
It pays to take turns doing hard jobs.

The geese honk from behind to encourage those up front to keep up their speed.

Teamwork Lesson:
An encouraging word goes a long way.

Finally, when a goose gets sick, or is wounded and falls out, two geese fall out of formation and follow him down to help and protect him.

Teamwork Lesson:
Loyalty helps individuals and strengthens the group.

A successful school can benefit from embracing these teamwork lessons. Let's look at some of the correlations:

1. **If we fly together**, we will all work less and benefit more. Unfortunately, if one person gets out of formation, the others will have to make up for the additional resistance.

2. **We need to take turns** doing the hard jobs. It always seems that the same people end up doing the dirty work. However, sometimes these people get tired or sick and someone else has to step up. We have all been there. The principal is talking about some new committee assignment and everyone has their head and eyes down, praying that they won't be called upon. I know we all have enough on our plates but we need to be able to say yes when it is our turn. Are you ready?

3. **We need to be honkers** who constantly spread the good news.

4. **Throughout the year,** opportunities will arise that allow you to be there for your colleagues. This is how we create a special place to work and learn.

18

THEY COME WITH BAGGAGE

*"The student is not an interruption of our work, the
student is the purpose of our work."*

—WILLIAM W. PURKEY

UNFORTUNATELY, TEACHING IN the early 21st century involves much more than just being an expert in a subject
area. Today's teachers must be counselors, nurses, psy-
chologists, motivational speakers, and magicians as well
as possess many other skills that they never tell you about
in the schools of teacher education.

Our students come to us with an enormous amount of
baggage. We don't know what happened last night, this
morning, or in between classes. Did Johnny just breakup
with his girlfriend? Has Julie eaten today? Is Billy's dad
still hitting him?

It is not enough for a teacher to just give out information and expect everyone to get it. If you are in tune to the
variety of issues facing your students, you are much better prepared to focus them for learning. However, when
we are so overwhelmed ourselves, we miss opportunities
to be there for our students. When we are unorganized,
we miss seeing their faces when they walk in, so we have
no idea that Becky was crying when she entered the classroom. Becky needs you!

We cannot control what happens outside of school.

However, it is our responsibility to create a little piece of heaven on earth within our classroom. Take pride in providing an environment that is comforting to your students. The greatest gift we can give our students is the knowledge that they have a caring, trusted adult that they can depend on every day. Sometimes, just being there can make all the difference.

Thanks for being there!

19

WE COME WITH BAGGAGE

"Never believe that a few caring people can't change the world. For, indeed, that's all who ever have."

—MARGARET MEAD

JUST LIKE STUDENTS come with baggage, it is important that people understand that teachers face the same human struggles that challenge all of us. As a principal, I try to be sensitive to the problems that many of my teachers are facing. I have been amazed recently by the number of teachers who have to miss work to take care of their elderly parents. Don't forget about the teachers who are experiencing the joy and challenge of raising young children. There can be nothing more stressful than having to pry your child off your leg as he/she begins a 7:00–4:00 day at daycare. This is why it is important to create an atmosphere that allows teachers to feel they are part of a family.

Have you ever tried to explain to someone else what we really do? I can never quite give it justice. Only we teachers really understand the unyielding barrage of interactions that make-up our day. If we counted the hours, we probably spend more time with our fellow teachers than we do with our own family. Throughout the school year, there will be several opportunities to reach out to colleagues in need. Sometimes, just a short note or kind gesture can help a teacher make it through the day.

Life is tough enough. If you have to work, at least it should be at a place that you enjoy and feel appreciated. Make sure you do your part to support your peers. You never know when you will need their help.

20

SCHOOL SPIRIT

"Live as if you were to die tomorrow. Learn as if you were to live forever."

—MAHATMA GANDHI

I RECENTLY WITNESSED one of the great American experiences, the high school football pep rally. As I looked across the packed gymnasium of 1,400 screaming 7-12 graders, I couldn't help but think about how school is much more than just books and lessons. School is about life. It is about building memories. Hopefully, for most of our students, the experience can be looked back upon as an enjoyable one.

Today, I saw a microcosm of an entire community. I saw black and white, old and young, 30 ACT's and 12 ACT's all united in support of their school. I was most touched by the teachers who participated in the pep rally. I see these teachers everyday in the classroom teaching their tails off. But, when I looked out and saw them doing a line dance to a country song blaring over the gym speakers and the kids screaming and cheering them on, I knew I was working at a special place. These teachers who are willing to let down their guard with an unabashed love for their school are truly difference-making educators. Show me a teacher who openly expresses a love for the school and I'll show you a teacher who will be more respected and loved by the students.

Extracurricular activities such as athletics, band, choir, and drama make-up a huge part of the school culture. Right or wrong, the community rallies behind these activities more than they do the academic performance of the students. For some reason, there is more emotion involved watching Johnny marching on the field with a trumpet, or Susie somersaulting through a cheerleading routine, or Reggie running for a touchdown than there is for Billy taking an algebra test. With this said, it is important that we as educators understand the values and life lessons that are taught in these endeavors.

School spirit is a critical component to any school. So often when teachers see one of their students in their own element (field of play, on stage, etc.) they begin to have a different perspective about them and a new avenue to reach them. Even if line dancing is not your thing, I challenge you to find ways to make sure the kids know you love your school. A teacher who participates and supports the many diverse activities of the school will have a much more enriching experience. The old Beach Boys' song "Be True to Your School" should be an anthem for every teacher.

21

LOYALTY

*"The difference between 'involvement' and 'commit-
ment' is like an egg-and-ham breakfast: the chicken was
'involved'- the pig was 'committed'."*

—ANONYMOUS

EVERY ORGANIZATION IS only as good as the people within
it. There are numerous traits needed to make a school
successful. A key ingredient is loyalty to the school. It
is so much easier to give your heart and soul to a school
that you are truly dedicated to.

I recently hired a math teacher. As is many times the
case, I felt good about her qualifications, but you are never quite sure how someone will fit in. At the first home
football game, I was running around taking care of ad-
ministrative duties when I saw the new math teacher vol-
unteering in the concession stand. I knew right away we
had found someone who had a chance to be more than
just an employee.

In today's educational environment, a teacher must
be an ambassador who sends out positive messages about
our schools. This loyalty should extend to what you say
about other members of the school staff. Even though
you may disagree with someone on the staff, you don't
have to make it public knowledge. There are enough people out there taking pot shots at the school and teachers.
Don't contribute to negative conversations. You never
know when you will be the topic.

22

PERFECT FOR RAISING A FAMILY

"One hundred years from now, it will not matter what my bank account was, how big my house was, or what kind of car I drove. But the world may be a little better, because I was important in the life of a child."

—FOREST WITCRAFT

I HAVE MENTIONED on numerous occasions that teaching is one of the most challenging jobs in America. However, without question, the most important and challenging job is the task of raising a family. Society, and in turn schools, continue to be impacted by the ever increasing percentage of homes without a father present and parents who are unable to stay home with their small children because of the need for two incomes.

My wife and I are both educators. We have experienced the stress of both of us teaching while trying to raise three small children. However, if you have to work, I can't think of a better job for raising a family. First, you have all the same vacation days with your children. Second, a factor that cannot be underestimated is the ability to keep up with who your children are hanging out with and how they are performing in school. Lastly, if we are honest, the car ride to and from school could possibly be the best quiet time we get with our children.

Being a working parent is tough enough. At least teaching is a profession that gives you an opportunity to stay involved in your children's life. You can't put a price on that.

Cost of field trip to pumpkin patch	$5.00
Girl Scout uniform	$75.00
Prom dress	$325.00
Knowing her date is not a psycho	Priceless

23

INTRODUCED VS. TAUGHT

"Give a man a fish and he will eat for a day. Teach a man to fish and he will eat for the rest of his life."

—CHINESE PROVERB

HERE IS AN interesting question. Have we really taught something if the students didn't learn it? Just introducing a topic or skill does not guarantee that it has been taught. It has been introduced, but only when retained and able to be used by the majority of the class can we say we have taught the skill. Researchers from the *National Training Laboratories* examined the impact of different instructional methods on the retention rate of student learners:

Average Retention Rate:

Lecture	5%
Reading	10%
Audio-visual	20%
Demonstration	30%
Discussion group	50%
Practice by doing	75%
Teaching others	90%

As educators, we should not be surprised by the research. You and I know that you really don't know anything until you have to teach it yourself. I thought I knew what mitosis was when I first started teaching. I passed the National Teachers Exam. But in reality, the first time I had to teach the process of cell division I was barely staying one step ahead of the kids.

How can we take this research and enhance our own instruction? Let's begin by moving away from our dependence on multiple choice/fill-in-the blank type evaluations and adopt more performance-based assessments where students have to show us what they really know. When challenged in this format, most students will rise to the occasion just like you and I did when we stayed one step ahead of our first class.

24

THE ULTIMATE SCHEDULE

"Time is the coin of your life. It is the only coin you have, and only you can determine how it will be spent. Be careful lest you let other people spend it for you."

—CARL SANDBURG

TO ME, THE school calendar is a divinely developed instrument. Maybe it's because I basically have been in school all my life, but the school schedule sure seems to fit my personality. I like to set small goals and then stay focused (with excellence) on them until collapsing across the finish line. Whether it is just a one-day holiday or a two-week vacation, I am usually excited about returning to school and attacking the next goal. For the past twenty-one years I have embraced the following educator goals:

Goal # 1	Make it to Labor Day
Goal # 2	Thanksgiving Holidays
Goal # 3	Christmas Holidays
Goal # 4	Martin Luther King Holiday
Goal # 5	Spring Break
Goal # 6	Easter Vacation
Goal # 7	Last Day of School

We have all heard the phrase "The best thing about teaching is June, July, and August." Even though this phrase could be construed as somewhat negative, and in many places school starts way too early in August, there is no doubt that summer vacation is a wonderful part of the teaching experience. Teaching requires a tremendous amount of work at home that most people do not see. Whether it is grading papers until midnight, cutting out letters for the bulletin board, or preparing lesson plans for the upcoming week, it is inevitable that some work will be done at home. Let us not forget that many teachers will spend their summer in workshops or college courses striving to improve their skills or to maintain their teaching certification. It is for these reasons and many others that we should not feel guilty for having what I consider to be the "Ultimate Schedule." Not only do we have a nice summer vacation, we also get two weeks off for Christmas, one week off for spring break, and many other one-day traditional holidays. These breaks come when we need them the most, and they allow us to recharge our batteries for one of the most demanding jobs on earth.

I'm not sure what the best thing about teaching is; however, June, July and August certainly rank high on the list.

25

CHARACTER COUNTS

"The ultimate measure of a man is not where he stands in moments of comfort, but where he stands at times of challenge and controversy."

—MARTIN LUTHER KING, JR.

TODAY, MORE THAN any other time in the history of our great country, we need leaders with moral integrity. As the lines of what society deems right and wrong become more and more blurred, teachers are uniquely positioned to fight the tide of moral decay. Students look to you for leadership. The everyday experience of the American classroom presents numerous opportunities to reinforce appropriate behaviors. Character building is too important to just turn our heads and say that it is someone else's job. The good teacher is always looking for the teachable moment. Sometimes it has nothing to do with the curriculum and everything to do with life and how we treat others. This is where we as teachers can make the biggest impact.

A few years ago our school adopted a definition of "Character" passionately presented by J.C. Watts, the former congressman from Oklahoma. Mr. Watts defined character as "Doing what's right, when nobody is looking." This simple but powerful message has become a standard of excellence that both students and teachers have strived to attain. As educators, we must live our lives in a way that gives us the credibility to lead young people through their formative years. If we don't, who will?

26

PLANNING PERIOD

"God grant me the serenity to accept the things I cannot change, the courage to change the things I can, and the wisdom to know the difference."

—REINHOLD NIEBUHR

LET ME BEGIN by saying that teachers certainly deserve more time during the day to plan lessons and activities. There is a particular injustice occurring in most elementary schools where elementary teachers are given just thirty minutes of planning time and spend their lunch eating with and supervising young children. What other profession in the world requires the employees to ask for help so someone can watch their class while they literally run to the restroom? With all this said, there are ways to use what little time you have more wisely.

It begins by simply starting a habit of visualizing the next day and organizing the items needed. Don't be caught by the "Law of the Copier." This law states that if one waits until the last minute to make copies, the copy machine will automatically jam and require major attention from the only person who knows how to fix it, the school secretary. All good teachers know that if you need something copied for the next day you better do it now or forever hold your peace. Each school day has enough moments where you are flying by the seat of your pants. By being proactive, you can relax enough to enjoy your evening and be better able to handle the next day's unannounced parent conference or crying child.

P.S. Please stay out of the teachers' lounge. There are not many teacher lounges out there that are filled with those who want to talk about how great this profession is and how wonderful the children are. Check your mailbox, grab a snack for energy, and then run out of there as fast as you can. There are other ways to have social interactions with your colleagues; the planning period is not one of them.

27

THE ULTIMATE QUESTION?

"What's good for the goose, is good for the gander."

—NOT SURE

HERE IS THE ultimate reflective question for any teacher. Would you want your own child in your class? There is no better judge than whether it is good enough for your own child. We are always quick to judge the assignments that other teachers give our children. Let us self analyze our own assignments using this same standard. The next time you give a class assignment or homework assignment, ask yourself whether you would be impressed if it was sent home by another teacher for your child to complete or would you think is was unchallenging busy work.

Is the atmosphere in your classroom the type that you would want your child to be a part of? Make this question the litmus test by which you conduct your classroom. If the answer is "yes" then everything else will take care of itself.

P. S. I hate to admit it, but I had to go to www.askjeeves. com to find out what a "gander" was. But, I think you get the point. You take care of my kids and I'll take care of yours. Let's both commit ourselves to excellence and treat all children like we would want our own to be treated.

28

THE NINETY-MINUTE CHALLENGE

"Nothing great was ever achieved without enthusiasm."

—RALPH WALDO EMERSON

THE EVER-INCREASING NUMBER of schools using the 4x4 or block schedule has forced teachers to examine the way they manage their classrooms. With research stating that fifteen to twenty minutes is the maximum attention span of young people, how do we create an effective ninety-minute class?

The first goal is to get out of survival mode and accept the challenge of creating a dynamic, well-organized lesson. Planning is the key. I suggest at least four different activities within each lesson. These activities can range from lecture to group work and just about everything in between, with no activity lasting more than twenty minutes.

Do you remember that Tuesday-Thursday college class that was an hour and fifteen minutes long? Remember how you thought you would die if you didn't get out of there? Do your students feel that way about your class? Please don't embrace the philosophy, "My teachers did it to me, so I am going to do it to you." Just because we suffered through poorly run classes does not make it okay to punish today's students. We owe our students ninety-minutes of high quality instruction. No excuses!

29

STAFF DEVELOPMENT

STAFF DEVELOPMENT HAS got to be one of the great enigmas in education today. There is nothing better than good staff development. There is nothing worse than bad staff development. Unfortunately, teachers have been exposed to so much bad staff development that they enter all training sessions with an attitude of gloom and doom. The truly professional teacher will approach all training opportunities with an open mind and a desire to gain something positive.

As is the case with all aspects of our lives, it all comes down to our attitude. If we expect to get nothing out of a training session then we will probably not. I challenge you to approach staff development with a positive attitude.

Let's make Charles Swindoll's reflection a guiding force in our daily lives.

Attitude

The longer I live, the more I realize the impact of attitude on life. Attitude, to me is more important than facts. It is more important than the past, than education, than money, than circumstances, than failures, than successes, than what other people think or say or do. It is more important than appearance, giftedness or skill. It will make or break a company...a church...a home. The remarkable thing is we have a choice everyday regarding the attitude we will embrace for that day. We cannot change our past...we cannot

change the fact that people will act in a certain way.
We cannot change the inevitable. The only thing we can
do is play on the one string we have, and that is our atti-
tude...I am convinced that life is 10% what happens to
me and 90% how I react to it. And so it is with you...we
are in charge of our attitudes.

—CHARLES SWINDOLL

P.S. When you are introduced to poor professional development, let your principal and superintendent respectfully hear from you. Unless teachers demand higher quality support, they are going to keep getting what they have always gotten.

30

STAYING ALIVE, STAYING ALIVE

"Beware how you take away hope from another human being."

—OLIVER WENDELL HOLMES

SOME OF YOU might be too young to remember the Bee Gee's and John Travolta in *Saturday Night Fever*; however, the idea of staying alive is what I want us to embrace when looking at the grades of some of our students.

I want you to make a special effort to target the "at-risk" students who failed your first nine-weeks or those who are failing second nine-weeks and do whatever it takes to keep them in the ballgame. A 42 or a 57 for the nine-weeks pretty much ends it for the year. If a student makes a 42 on a unit test, then make him/her take it over until they show you mastery. How dare a student make a 42 on your test! Take it personally.

Good teaching is just like good coaching. It takes relationship building and motivation to get the most out of your players. The goal is to invest so much into your students that the students don't want to let you down. No one said it was going to be easy, but we must try to reach every child. We will be exhausted, but that is what Christmas holidays and summer vacation are for.

31

REALITY TV

*"Knowledge of the self is the mother of all knowledge.
So it is incumbent on me to know myself, to know it
completely."*

—Kahlil Gibran

DO WE REALLY want to become a better teacher? Are we
aware of our effectiveness in the classroom? Are you willing to sincerely evaluate yourself? There is only one way
to truly discover these answers. Videotape yourself con-
ducting your class.

The old adage "The camera never lies" is a truth that
can lead to self-reflection and ultimately instructional improvement. I believe the most powerful tool for teacher
improvement is the use of videotape for self-analysis. As
an administrator and consultant, I have had the privilege
of speaking in front of numerous audiences. Many times I
have had these presentations videotaped and found it to be
extremely valuable to review the tape for ways to improve
my speaking skills. Inevitably, I will pick up small details
that will make my next presentation better. I want to be
an outstanding public speaker. To achieve this goal, I must
be my own worst critic. It should be no different for the
classroom teacher.

If teachers will videotape themselves and honestly
evaluate the tape, they will see things that no other method can reveal. The tape is excellent for reviewing the ef-

fectiveness of one's voice, body language, questioning techniques, student interactions, flow of the lesson, and numerous other teaching skills. I challenge any teacher who really wants to improve to incorporate the use of this simple, but powerful tool.

32

AM I THE PROBLEM?

"You cannot escape the responsibility of tomorrow by evading it today."

—ABRAHAM LINCOLN

MY FIRST EDUCATION job was as a biology teacher and coach at St. Paul High School in Covington, Louisiana. St. Paul's was a great place to work. As a matter of fact, their motto is "St. Paul's: A Great Place to Grow Up." I know I did a great deal of growing up during those first years of teaching. It was during these years that I was introduced to the tenets of William Glasser's "Reality Therapy." Our assistant principal, Mrs. Merle Dooley, was an advocate of Glasser's philosophy and incorporated many staff development activities based on his teachings. I don't remember all the principles; however, there was one aspect of Reality Therapy that stuck with me. Glasser taught that when dealing with student discipline problems the first thing a teacher must do is stop and ask, What have I done to contribute to the problem? When I first heard this philosophy, I was turned off by it. If a student is misbehaving in class, how can I be the problem? As I have gotten older and not only experienced problems in my own classroom but have handled literally thousands of discipline referrals sent to my office from other teachers, I have come to see the wisdom in Glasser's first step.

There are usually many reasons why a student acts out

in a classroom. The mature, confident teacher is willing to evaluate whether they could have played a role in the problem. Were my instructions confusing? Did I embarrass the student with my comments? Asking these types of questions and honestly answering them can sometimes shed a new light on the problem. Don't be afraid to ask the tough question. Am I part of the problem?

33

Don't Walk on Eggshells

"Life affords no greater responsibility, no greater privilege, than raising of the next generation."

—C. Everett Koop

When it comes to running a school, classroom, or any organization, someone has to be in charge. Make sure that in your classroom that someone is YOU. You cannot walk around tiptoeing like you're walking on eggshells. Part of your job is to tell students what to do and when to do it.

In today's society, schools, teachers, and administrators are often the last bastions of responsibility and accountability. If we do not hold students to high standards, who will? Many parents today are so overwhelmed by the challenge of raising children that they basically let them do what they want to do. You and I are given the task of having to say things to students that they are not accustomed to hearing. These include words and phrases like "No" or "Do it again, this is not good enough," or "I need you to do this and please do it now."

We need dedicated educators who understand the importance of being a voice of discipline for young people. We also need leaders who earn the opportunity to discipline through the creation of an atmosphere of dignity and mutual respect. By creating this type of environment and clearly communicating your expectations, there will be no question who is in charge. Thanks for being strong, consistent, and caring!

34

No Child Left Behind

"We need to believe that all children can learn, but then what we need to act on is changing the word "can" to "will".

—Michael Feinberg

How can you have a conversation about education in the early 21st century and not mention *"No Child Left Behind"*? This federal legislation was passed by Congress and signed by President George Bush on January 8, 2002. It has become one of the most influential educational initiatives in United States history.

As a school principal during the initial implementation of this legislation, I was charged like my other colleagues across the country with the challenge of understanding the many requirements of NCLB. Terms like "highly qualified teachers" and "percentage of students who are proficient in reading, language, and math" became part of my vocabulary.

Even though I am not a fan of additional bureaucracy and federal intrusion into the local issues of public education, I have become concerned with the negative connotation that many teachers and administrators have attached to NCLB.

In its purest form, what can be wrong with making sure that no child is left behind in our efforts to educate all children? I have learned as a supervisor of other adults that it is human nature that "what gets checked, gets done" and if you don't check it, many times it does not get done. Setting up an accountability system that insures that we are examining the learning performances of all students is a sound educational practice. If we are honest with ourselves, prior to NCLB, we got the test scores back, took a quick look, and went back to doing what we had always done. We looked at the scores from the big picture angle and seldom got down to the individual level to determine who was falling behind and how we could immediately intervene to prevent the loss of a child.

I am not sure if we will be able to get 100 percent of our students proficient in reading, language, and math by 2014 as mandated by NCLB. However, there is no question that we now have children in remediation programs across the United States that would not be getting this extra attention if it had not been for this new system of "checking to see if it is getting done."

Even with all its faults, most would agree that *No Child Left Behind* has caused us to raise the bar and bring our "A" game. Isn't this what our students deserve?

35

You Can't Fool Kids

"Go out and preach the gospel, and use words if you have to."

—St. Francis of Assisi

There is no more astute animal than a human child. Just sit back and listen to them. Whether it is your own children in the backseat of the car or just some students talking in the cafeteria, the wisdom and honesty they display can be quite enlightening. When discussing their teachers, they will sometimes miss the mark, but much more often they are right on the money.

You can't trick kids. They know whether we are prepared for class, know our material, and want to be there or not. Most importantly, they know whether we genuinely care for them or not. We all have our good and bad days. Just make sure that after 180 days of sharing a class together, your students can say without hesitation that you were prepared, passionate, and compassionate. If you have these three traits, students will know they were in the presence of a true educator.

36

THE NEXT GREAT GENERATION

"The future belongs to those who believe in the beauty of their dreams."

—ELEANOR ROOSEVELT

TOM BROKAW OF NBC news has done a fabulous job reminding us of the courage and sacrifices of the American people during World War II. Brokaw has rightfully named them the "Greatest Generation." As I walk daily on a campus of 1,400 seventh through twelve graders, I choose to believe that they have a chance to be the "Next Great Generation."

I believe there are two groups out there today: the PESSIMISTS who believe that education is falling apart and that schools are filled with terrible kids and teachers and the OPTIMISTS who see the unlimited potential in today's youth and believe that these are great times to be a part of education. I happen to be an optimist and hope that you will join me in this group.

Let's compare today's graduate with the graduate from the previous generation. As hard as it is to admit, I think I will qualify as someone from the previous generation. Most of my education was acquired in the seventies. Now, thirty years later, I am in charge of creating a high school graduate that can excel in the 21st century. Let's look at today's graduate.

First, they will have earned probably five or six more

credits than you or I did. This equates into almost a whole extra year of education. Secondly, their access to technology is amazing. Many of our graduates are leaving high school with skills that give them a true advantage over most of the current workforce. Whether it be power point presentations, tech prep introductions to lasers and robotics, or an increased emphasis on oral communication, I don't think there is any question that today's students are much better educated than I was. The key is to motivate students to take advantage of these opportunities. This is why we need educators who can communicate to young people in a way that motivates them to reach their highest potential. The sky is the limit.

Thanks for believing in our kids!

37

THE PARENT TRAP

"Success on any major scale requires you to accept responsibility... in the final analysis, the one quality that all successful people have... is the ability to take on responsibility."

—MICHAEL KORDA

TO CALL OR not to call, this is the question. I recently had a parent in my office literally in tears over the grades her son had earned. She was frustrated and felt like the teachers did not care. She based her view on the fact that well into the third nine-weeks, her son was failing every class and not one teacher had called her to discuss ways to improve the situation. Now I know our teachers care. I witness their preparation and dedication to our young people every day. However, why had they not called? The decision to contact parents about the classroom performance of their children is a constant struggle. Sending letters home can be effective; however, a phone call can be much more informative and personal. The following is a list of reasons why I believe teachers don't call home:

1. **Not enough time:** School time is scarce and home time is precious and hectic.

2. **"It's not going to change anything."** We can't adopt this attitude.

3. **The dreaded ugly phone call.** It doesn't take but one of these to turn a teacher off.

4. **Poor phone skills.** Some people are not comfortable in this format.

All of these reasons and many more are very legitimate, but can they stand up to the ultimate litmus test? Would we want the teacher to call us if our own child was performing this way? I believe most of us would appreciate the call. It has been my experience that most phone calls home are well received. There is a skill to calling parents and making them feel at ease about your intent and concerns. Some suggestions:

1. **Try to keep it short and sweet** (literally).

2. **Start with positive comments.**

3. **List specific incidents.**

4. **Give hope, but express urgent need for change.**

5. **Solicit the parent's help.**

We owe parents at least one phone call to express our concerns with the way a failing or misbehaving child is performing. Don't wait until it is too late. Call today!

38

CAN WE WATCH A VIDEO?

"Good teaching is one-fourth preparation and three-fourths pure theatre."

—GAIL GODWIN

THE INTRODUCTION OF the TV/VCR into the classroom is one of the great technological advances in educational history. Nothing can bring the concept of plate tectonics alive like a video showing the actual footage of a volcano erupting. In today's MTV world, the use of videotapes to teach a concept is a must if we want to reach our students. I believe the proper use of videos can truly enhance a classroom. Unfortunately, I am concerned that educational videos are not being used in an effective manner. Too often they are used for the entire class period and within twenty minutes half the class is asleep. Also, many times the only assignment for the substitute is to put in the video and everyone be quiet. Even if these are excellent videos, the way we present them reduces their effectiveness and sends a message that this material is not important. The following is a list of techniques that will make the use of videos more effective:

1. Never show more than twenty minutes at a time. (Attention span)

2. After watching the entire video yourself, pick out small segments that fit perfectly with your lesson. You don't

have to show the whole tape when you know the part that is most important.

3. Use the remote control to stop the tape periodically for comments or questions. This keeps them awake.

4. Accountability: Have the students take notes during the tape, give a quiz at the end of the video, incorporate test questions based on the tape. If you do this consistently, students will know that you feel this information is important.

Educational videos can play a vital role in a teacher's instructional repertoire. The above suggestions will hopefully increase the effectiveness of this instructional tool.

39

It's All About the Dash

*"We make a living by what we get. We make a life by
what we give."*

—Sir Winston Churchill

A PERSON (1958-2042) is born in 1958 and dies in 2042.
The important thing is not the birth or death, but what
the person does in between (the dash) that matters. For
the teacher, this time was spent giving back to the community.

I have great respect for those who give of their time
and talents to serve on mission trips to Africa, Russia,
Mexico, and other needy areas of the world. As teachers,
we have our own mission, and we are saving lives every
day. The life of a teacher is the equivalent of a thirty-year
"mission trip." The true missionaries are not looking for
rewards or recognition. They serve because they have a
calling to make a difference.

If you have been in this business long enough, you
already know that students seldom tell us "thank you for
making a difference in my life." After twenty years, I can
still count on one hand the times a student has actually
come up and said "thank you." However, just one walk
through the mall during Christmas season and I am re-
minded of why I love being an educator. Everywhere I
go, I hear "Hey! Coach Benigno" or "Hey! Dr. B." You see,
when you treat students with respect and work to develop

relationships with them, you enjoy seeing them in the mall or at the grocery store. The ultimate thrill is seeing a student that you wondered whether he/she would ever make it or not and there the student is functioning in this crazy society. You don't have to go to Africa or Mexico. There are kids who need you right here in (Soso, Eatonville, or Back Bay) your hometown.

Thank you for making a difference!

40

THANKS FOR THE RIDE

"Destiny is not a matter of chance, it is a matter of choice; it is not a thing to be waited for, it is a thing to be achieved."

—WILLIAM JENNINGS BRYAN

ON A FRIDAY night in December of 2005, I was on a cold and damp football field listening to our coaches' talk to their players after the game. We had just lost the Mississippi South State Football Championship for the third straight year. To be one win away from the state championship game for three years in a row and to come up empty was an emotional and draining experience for our players, coaches, and community.

With a tear in many an eye, the coaches shared with the players how much they appreciated their dedication and effort and told them "thanks for the ride." As I went to prepare the following Monday's memo for my staff, it hit me that just like the football players, we were about to reach halftime of our "Great Ride."

The 180-day journey of a school year requires the same dedication and effort that the players give each practice and Friday night. The problem is that for us "every day is game day." We must strive for excellence in every instructional moment that we have. Just like the coaches tell the players to give everything they have and leave it all on the field, I challenge you to leave no stone unturned in your effort to reach all the kids entrusted to your care.

At the end of our season (May 25th), I want you and your students to be able to look each other in the eye (maybe with tears) and say, "thanks for the ride."

41

CELEBRATE SUCCESS

"Don't judge each day by the harvest you reap but by the seeds that you plant."

—ROBERT LOUIS STEVENSON

JANUARY 24, 1999 was a big day in the Benigno family. Our youngest daughter, Kaitlin, rode her bike by herself for the first time. Oh, you should have seen the gleam in her eye as she realized that I was no longer holding onto her sweatshirt. It was so hard to let go of that sweatshirt. I ran along side of her, nervous to death that she might fall and hurt herself. At the end of the bike ride, we celebrated with a big hug and congratulations.

Our classrooms are filled with opportunities to run along side our students holding tightly to their sweatshirts. When we finally let go and they succeed on their own, celebrate the achievement. Whether it is the completion of a math problem, the survival of an oral presentation, or the return of a good test grade, take advantage of the opportunity to praise and motivate your students. It is this reinforcement that can give them the determination to overcome the next time they skin their knee.

42

THE SENIOR YEAR

*"Americans will always do the right thing, after ex-
hausting every other possibility."*

—SIR WINSTON CHURCHILL

I WONDER IF Winston Churchill would feel this way if he
were to evaluate our public schools? In many areas, the
public education system of the United States needs to exhaust every possibility. Think of all the changes that have
occurred in the 20th century. If one were to fall asleep in
1905 and wake up 100 years later in 2005, the one institu-
tion that would look almost the same would be the American classroom.

So if we agree with Winston Churchill, then let's finally do the right thing and change the way we prepare
students for the 21st century workforce and especially the
"wasted year" of the high school senior. Most high school
seniors across America spend their time trying to figure
out how they can take the fewest classes possible and get
off campus as fast as they can. By the time Christmas rolls
around, the valedictorian has been named and rank in class
determined, and the rest of the year is spent counting the
days to graduation. This disease called "senioritis" de-
serves a cure. It will require new thinking from educators
to make sure that our last chance to touch them before
they enter the real world is a productive, challenging, and
relevant experience.

I don't have all the answers. However, I have been an advocate for *senior projects* (www.seniorproject.net) as a way to establish a capstone performance for students who are about to walk across the stage and into the real world.

In 2001, the National Commission on the Senior Year published their findings in a preliminary report entitled "*The Lost Opportunity of the Senior Year: Finding a better way.*" This report highlighted senior projects as an example of the additional rigor needed in the senior year of high school. Senior projects allow students to truly show us what they know. You've been in school twelve years. What can you really do? This culminating assignment allows students to pick a topic of their choice and then become an expert in that area. It usually includes a research paper and the development of a product or project that is an extension of their research, and then culminates with a presentation in front of a panel of judges from the community.

Whether it be senior projects, dual enrollment at the local community college, or community service requirements, we must make the senior year a different experience. If not, we will continue to have students disengaged from learning and floundering through one of the most important times of their lives.

43

DRESS FOR SUCCESS

"The advantage of looking professional is that it keeps you from self-destructing in the first few seconds, before the students make any hasty judgments about you."

—DR. HARRY WONG

EACH DAY WE announce to the world how we feel about our profession and ourselves. The most outward sign of this expression is how we dress. Like it or not, people make judgments about us based on how we look. In a business where respect is a major key to success, we must do everything we can to look professional. Taking pride in your appearance sends a positive message to the students and community.

In many ways, teaching is a daily performance on stage. When you look good, you feel good. This feeling of confidence and self-esteem can only help us as we deal with the challenges of motivating young people.

In our teacher handbook, I simply state that teachers are expected to dress professionally. I am not looking for conformity or the reduction of individuality. However, take a look in the mirror and honestly access the image you are projecting. It is never too late to change.

44

NEVER GIVE UP ON THEM

"The difference between those who fail and those who succeed is largely perseverance. Never Quit."

—CHARLES SCHWAB

WORKING WITH CHILDREN is a wonderful study of human nature. How can you love them so much one-minute and want to strangle them the next? As mentioned earlier (see #5), it is important that we look through the lens of the child and try to remember what it was like at that age.

As a middle school principal, one reason for my success and current sanity is that I clearly remember how goofy and silly my friends and I were at twelve and thirteen years old. We got our tails paddled many a time. We were worried about girls, football, and then fractions and verb usage. Today, Brehm is a lawyer, Mark is the president of an oil drilling company, and I have a Ph.D in educational leadership. It is interesting to note that none of our parents had a college degree and we were the first in our families to receive a degree. I sure am glad our teachers did not give up on us.

As a teacher, coach, and principal, I have had the privilege of working with thousands of students. I have seen time and time again examples of young people whose behaviors and attitudes were enough to drive you crazy. It would have been so easy to give up on them. They take up so much of your energy and attention. However, these are the ones who need us the most. When we refuse to give up on them and continue to counsel with dignity and respect, the rewards can be huge.

As we continue to establish our body of work and more and more of our students grow up and become adults, we hear about Jacob, who would sit in my office and tell me, "Call the cops, I don't care, the number is 425-0270." Jacob just completed his GED and says he wants to be a lawyer. What about James, who would cuss like a sailor when he was sent to my office and now he is in high school and can't walk by me without going out of his way to shake my hand? I can see in his eyes that without saying it, he is telling me that he is doing well and thanking me for not giving up on him. What about Donna, who would fight at the drop of a hat and now she is making straight A's in high school? What about Murray, who we had to chase into the parking lot more than once. He was running home because, "he hated this school and everybody in it"? Murray recently came up to me in the mall and told me all about his construction job and his new wife and baby. I could go on and on. This is why we teach. This is why we can sleep at night because we know we have made a difference in the lives of children.

May God bless you as you find the next Jacob, James, Donna, and Murray.

45

TAKE CARE OF MY BABY

"After the verb 'to Love,' 'to Help' is the most beautiful verb in the world."

—BERTHA VON SUTTNER

HOPEFULLY, THE EARLIER pages of this book have clearly captured my respect for all educators and the tremendous role teachers play in the lives of students. As an educator, I have spent over twenty years working with students in grades seven through twelve. Even though I have great admiration for all of my colleagues in secondary education, I must say that it is even a more special calling to be an elementary teacher. These educators work with our most vulnerable children at a time when their learning potential is growing at warp speed.

If you analyze the keys to future learning, it becomes evident that the ability to read and comprehend, along with multiplication tables and fractions, are the foundational bedrocks for success at the secondary level. Elementary teachers who juggle many hats on a daily basis are responsible for teaching these vital developmental skills. I would venture to say that if you had ten elementary teachers and ten secondary teachers switch places for a week, eight of the ten elementary teachers would enjoy the pace of the secondary teacher's day, while only one of ten secondary teachers would want any part of going back to the elementary school. With this unproven theory as a backdrop,

I want to thank all the elementary teachers who take care of our babies.

My wife and I are currently raising three wonderful children who are the ages of seventeen, fifteen and seven. For those who have children, isn't it amazing how they can come from the same parents and be so different? We are very blessed. However, our seven-year-old little boy is in first grade, and he has some significant phonological processing problems. His verbal vocabulary qualifies him for the gifted program, yet his reading skills qualify him for an IEP in speech/language.

As educators, we knew this was a pivotal year for him to find some way to learn how to read. We were really scared. Then, we got the best of all blessings. We ended up with Mrs. Cyndy as his first grade teacher. As we have said throughout this book, the teacher can make all the difference in the world. This wonderful lady embraced the challenge of teaching our son. She identified the problem and proceeded to change her teaching methods to best reach our child. She loved, disciplined, challenged, and nurtured him in a way that made him feel special. He is now riding in the back seat of our car using his association method skills to sound out every word on every sign in Laurel, Mississippi. He is going to be a reader, and we thank God every day for bringing Mrs. Cyndy into our lives. This life-giving instruction is happening every day in elementary classrooms across America.

Thanks for taking care of our babies!

46

SOMEONE HAS TO LOVE THEM

"I don't know what your destiny will be, but one thing I do know: the only ones among you who will be really happy are those who have sought and found how to serve."

—ALBERT SCHWEITZER

THEY SURE DO make it hard, but someone has to love the middle school students. When I introduce myself as a middle school principal, I usually describe my job as someone who basically chases 500 seventh and eighth graders every day. People proceed to say things like: "Oh, bless your heart" or "Better you, than me" and I go on to remind them that someone has to love them.

The middle school world is a fascinating mixture of hormones and energy that requires a special type of educator. I know I may sound sick, but I really do enjoy working with this age group. They are old enough to mess with and joke around with, but young enough that they still let you love on them. Even more interesting is the range of student development both physically and emotionally found within the walls of a typical middle school. These twelve to fifteen year olds come in all shapes and sizes. I am always amazed on the first day of school when I see the new seventh graders and they look like such babies and last year's seventh graders who are now in eighth grade look like grown people. What an incredible time of change. Unfortunately, this period of rapid change makes them one of the most vulnerable and needy of all students.

These creatures require a combination of drill sergeant, psychotherapist, and mind reader. They can forget things faster than you can say "pizza and fries." They are unorganized, loud, obnoxious and sweet, all at the same time. What is most irritating is that they cannot keep their hands to themselves. Occasionally, I am stuck on the phone when the bell to exchange classes rings and I end up having to watch the security camera view of the hall while I am finishing my conversation. This camera angle gives you an interesting insight to the potential trauma of traveling a middle school hall between classes. If you will just watch for sixty seconds, you will see more punching, popping, and silliness than you ever care to see. In general, no one is being mean. They are just playing. Unfortunately, they play all the time and when told to stop, they will usually do so until the next class exchange. Then it starts all over again. So, how do we create an atmosphere of excellence instead of just surviving this most challenging of age groups?

First of all, let's make sure they have as much structure as possible. When given too much leeway, they will destroy the best of teachers. As mentioned earlier, it must start on the very first day of school or the rest of the year will be a living nightmare. The following formula gives you a chance to succeed:

$$\frac{\textbf{Bellwork} \text{ (zip and walk)}}{\textbf{Seating Chart} \text{ (no roll call)}} \times \frac{\textbf{Teacher Movement}}{\textbf{High Expectations}}$$

Secondly, constantly evaluate your directions and procedures through the lens of "could this possibly confuse them" because if you leave it up to their assumptions, you will get twenty-five different products in each class. Third, and most importantly, never give up on them. They are going to test you and make you want to run to the nearest "Happy Hour." However, it never fails. Just when you are about to say, "I have had enough," one of them will warm your heart in a way that makes it all worthwhile.

Dr. James Dobson of *Focus on the Family* has a true passion for the human experience. His following commentary captures the emotion of being a middle school student:

> *I remember sitting one day in my car at a fast food restaurant eating a hamburger and french fries. When I looked in the rear view mirror, I saw the most pitiful, scrawny, dirty little kitten on a ledge behind my car. I was so touched by how hungry he looked, that I got out, tore off a piece of my hamburger and tossed it to him. But before this little kitten could reach it, a huge gray tomcat sprang out of the bushes, grabbed the morsel and gobbled it down. I felt so sorry for the little guy who turned and ran back into the shadows, still hungry and frightened. I was immediately reminded of my years as a junior high school teacher. I saw teenagers every day, who were just as needy, just as deprived, just as lost as that little kitten. It wasn't food that they required, it was love and attention and respect that they needed, and they were desperate for it. And just when they opened up and revealed the pain inside, one of the more popular kids would abuse them and ridicule them and send them scurrying back into the shadow, frightened and alone.*
>
> *We, as adults, must never forget the pain of trying to grow up and of the competitive world in which many adolescents live today. To take a moment to listen, to care, and to direct such a youngster may be the best investment of a lifetime.*

47

THE BIGGEST CHALLENGE

*"There are two ways of exerting one's strength: one is
pushing down, the other is pulling up."*

—BOOKER T. WASHINGTON

LOOK ACROSS YOUR classroom. Can there be a more diverse
collection of talents and interests? One of the biggest
challenges facing a teacher is how to deliver instruction
to such a diverse audience. How can you help all of them
reach their potential? It is a truly daunting task. Many
times we end up just teaching to the middle and hoping
for the best.

When we teach to the middle, who gets hurt the most?
Is it the advanced student who is bored out of his mind?
Or is it the slow student who is lost as a goose? The American public education system could be compared to the Disney classic, *Beauty and the Beast.* We are beautiful because
we try to teach all students. We are ugly because we try to
teach all students the same way at the same time. Even before *No Child Left Behind* and the new emphasis on school
accountability, there was always the pressing dilemma of
how to reach students with such a wide range of needs.
The most effective teachers are cognizant of this challenge and constantly strive to "differentiate instruction"
in a way that engages all learners.

Differentiating instruction is not creating more work
for the brightest and less work for the struggling stu-

dent. It is an effort to use various modes of instruction and student grouping to challenge all learners in the class. Picture a math class where the previous day the teacher had introduced a new concept (Ex. order of operations). The next day, instead of having all twenty students do the same worksheet, the teacher allows those who are comfortable with the concept to work the review problems while the five lowest students are pulled in a circle around the teacher getting in-depth instruction. Students who complete the worksheet are allowed to go to the computer for enhanced work. Congratulations, you have just differentiated instruction! It is difficult to do every day. Nevertheless, today the lower kids won. Next time, the lower kids are on the computer while you assist the advanced kids who are being challenged by a special word problem. Today, the advanced kids win.

Carol Ann Tomlinson, author of *The Differentiated Classroom: Responding to the Needs of All Learners* talks about the importance of content, process, and product. I am not an expert in this area, but I do believe in its premise. With this in mind, here is my simplified and hopefully stress-free version of "differentiated instruction."

Content: All students are introduced to the main concept. Through grouping, stations, and varied resources, the concept can be explored at different levels of complexity.

Process: The delivery of information and the activities used to guide learning are modified to allow for those who have a strong base to explore at deeper levels (advanced text, web searches, teach others) while those with a limited initial knowledge can be directed at a more appropriate pace.

Product: One of the best ways to engage all learners is to provide a variety of outlets for students to show what they know. Teachers who allow students to explore concepts in a way that fits their learning and interest styles are much more likely to see students shine. There is something about having options that eliminates excuses. Students can show mastery of the causes of the Revolutionary War through various methods. These could include a research paper, poster board presentation, rap song, or multiple-choice test. Bottom line, can they capture the essence of why America went to war with Britain?

There are certainly times for students to be sitting in rows, all hearing the same thing from the teacher. However, for them to be open for learning, today's students need to be stimulated through a variety of senses. Let us be open to exploring different ways to serve the diverse talents in our class.

Thanks for accepting the challenge!

48

HIGH STAKES TESTING

When we do the best we can, we never know what
miracle is wrought in our life, or in the life of another.

—HELEN KELLER

I KNOW THERE is a lot of stress out there about state test-ing and the requirements of *No Child Left Behind.* I have spent the last four years working with a group of won-derful teachers as we strived to become a Level 5 school. In Mississippi, a Level 5 school (Superior Performing) is the highest ranking an individual school can receive. We started as a Level 3 (Successful) school. After our first year together, we moved to a Level 4 (Exemplary) school, and then after the second year we became a Level 5 school. We have currently moved back to a Level 4 school. It is a constant challenge.

I know it is hard to do, but try not to get stressed out over the scores. All you can do is your best. However, we need to be constantly evaluating to make sure we really are giving our best effort. If we truly care and we are try-ing to be positive as we look for ways to help our students become proficient in the tested areas, then that is all we can really do. The following three questions need to drive your self-evaluation:

1. **Where are we?** (knowing the current status of stu-dents mastery of curriculum)

2. **Where are we going?** (understanding of pacing needed to cover all objectives)

3. **Who needs help getting there?** (knowledge of students who are struggling)

With these questions as a guide, we can focus on planning quality lessons and remediation for those who are at-risk.

The end of year state test has become the new final exam. We have always given final exams to determine whether our students have mastered the year's material. It is really not that different. By now, most of us know the design of the state test and have the resources we need to get the students ready for the test. Create a positive atmosphere and teach your tail off. That is all we can do.

49

WHAT'S WRONG WITH THIS PICTURE?

Education is an ornament in prosperity and a refuge in adversity.

—ARISTOTLE

IT IS 2:00 in the morning and someone is breaking into your house. A fire breaks out and your home is engulfed in flames. It is 7:00 a.m. and your child gets on a bus to spend the next eight hours with educators. Each of these images involves serious issues dealing with the most important aspects of your life.

What is interesting and sad is that when you call the policeman, fireman, or educator, you are calling the least paid people in our community. What does it say about our society that those charged with protecting our most valuable assets are compensated so poorly? I know we don't do it for the money. Nevertheless, it is a sad commentary on the priorities of our world. With all this said, there are ways to enhance your earning power and level of respect.

1. **More education = more money.** Most salary scales reward additional degrees. Also, additional degrees can prepare you for higher paying jobs within education.

2. **National Board Certification:** Most states have allocated stipends for those teachers who earn certification from the National Board for Professional Teaching Standards. In Mississippi, teachers can earn

an additional $6,000 a year. Achieving NBCT status also signifies a level of excellence that is recognized nationally.

3. **Understand** and **embrace** the test score challenge. I have a feeling that at some point, teachers whose students perform well on standardized test will be properly compensated.

4. **Be professional.** Our dress and conduct can go a long way toward changing the community's attitude toward teachers.

50

ROAD MAP FOR SUCCESS

Blessed are those who can give without remembering,
and take without forgetting.

—ELIZABETH BIBESCO

IT DOESN'T TAKE but one walk through Books-A-Million to know that Dr. John Maxwell is a one of America's leading authorities on leadership. I enjoy reading his books and subscribe to his e-mail service (www.injoy.com) which sends out a newsletter called "Leadership Wired." In his January 2005 addition, Dr. Maxwell shares some of the defining decisions that have shaped his life. Maxwell says he has decided:

1. **To continue to grow personally throughout his life.**

2. **To give and serve on the front end.** (Give with no strings attached)

3. **To exhibit a great attitude regardless of the situation.**

These same traits can serve as a road map for the difference-making educator. By constantly growing, serving, and exhibiting a positive attitude, we create an atmosphere of excellence that touches all that we come in contact with.

Let us join Dr. Maxwell on this journey toward excellence.

51

WHY SO EARLY?

It is common sense to take a method and try it. If it fails, admit it frankly and try another. But above all, try something.

—FRANKLIN D. ROOSEVELT

WHAT GETS YOU out of bed in the morning? I have a phrase I use that helps me to get out of bed in the morning. I remind myself, "You gotta be a big boy." Like Peter Pan, many of us would like to avoid the requirements of being an adult. Unfortunately, we have to work. However, why do we start school so early? Who came up with this idea? I love the opening scene from *Mr. Holland's Opus*. It depicts him getting out of bed for his first day as a teacher. As his wife rouses him out of bed, he wanders toward the bathroom sink. Looking into the mirror with sleepy eyes, he asks his wife "What time do I have to be there?" and she yells out 7:30. He gets this look of disgust and says, "What kind of people go to work at 7:30 in the morning?" It is a heck of a question. Are we sick or what? Many teachers have to be at school well before 7:00 a.m. There must be a better way.

There is a great deal of research that advocates starting school later in an effort to help students learn more and be healthier. Researchers from the University of Minnesota's Center for Applied Research and Educational Improvement worked with the Minneapolis Public School

District to explore the impact of later starting times on high school students. The schools involved changed their starting time of 7:15 a.m. to 8:40 a.m. Schools with the later start time reported improved grades and a decrease in tardiness, sleeping in class, and depression. Teachers and administrators observed that students seemed more alert, and the atmosphere of the school was calmer and more positive. This research seems to coincide with a more powerful research tool (common sense) that says, "Who in their right mind wants to get up at 5:00 or so to get ready for the day?"

If we are looking for another reason to not feel guilty about having the summer off, I say we use getting to work insanely early as one of our main justifications.

Good night and don't forget to set your alarm.

52

BURNED OUT OR BORED OUT?

Boring: To tire with dullness or repetition

—WEBSTER'S DICTIONARY

I ONCE HEARD someone say, "Teachers don't get burned out, they get bored out." I think there is a lot of wisdom in this opinion. I have seen several cases over the years where teachers who were becoming stale and indifferent about teaching all of a sudden caught their second wind and became passionate ambassadors for education due to some new idea or program that they embraced. In most of these cases, the new idea or project required the teacher to work harder than ever before. However, the excitement of adding something of quality to your repertoire can be truly invigorating.

The real key to success is making sure you are getting better every year. As long as you can see steady progress and can reflect on the things that you are now doing that you didn't do last year, then you should feel a level of achievement that keeps you coming back for more. We recently added an e-mail system to our campus. In just a matter of weeks we became e-mailing machines. We are now so much more efficient and communicative. This kind of small, yet substantial improvement keeps me passionate about the organization and its future.

In another example, I recently witnessed a fabulous transformation among our two seventh grade math teachers. Because of their willingness to embrace new instructional approaches, these wonderful teachers have taken their game to a new level. Their use of a new software program in conjunction with SmartBoard technology has made their classes engaging and fresh. During her annual teacher evaluation, one of them admitted that she had been feeling stale and wondered if teaching was what she wanted to continue to do. She then lit up as she talked about the impact of these new tools. She is on fire, and I have no doubt that she will ride this wave for several years. I was excited for her and most importantly for her students. They will be in the presence of an energized teacher who is no longer bored.

Teaching is a collection of routines that in many ways become the rhythm of our lives. However, if we are not careful, this rhythm will lull us to sleep and our work will become unfulfilling. To stay fresh, you must shock yourself with new challenges and activities. You still have a lot more in the tank than you realize. I challenge you to shake up your routine and get back to enjoying the ride. Here are a few suggestions:

1. **Change up your bellwork:** Don't let this vital class starting procedure become the same old, same old. There is nothing better than an awesome bellwork to start class. Bring in current events or use scenarios that require students to reflect on issues that will lead to lively topics that you are passionate about. Plan a week of perfect pre-bell activities and before you know it the bell will be ringing and you are wondering where the time went.

2. **Find a way to incorporate music** into your lessons. Music is the universal language. Wouldn't you have loved a teacher who found a way to have music in the class? Enough said.

3. **Create an oasis:** Your room does not have to be drab and plain. Rearrange the room, bring in plants and flowers, and fill your walls with motivational messages.

4. **Plan a get away:** You and a colleague need to establish an annual trip to an educational conference that offers educational data as well as great shopping, golfing, and good food. What a perfect way to stay fresh and enthused.

5. **Read and reflect:** Subscribe to a monthly educational journal that allows you time to reflect on the latest trends and issues in education. Information = Power

6. **Short videos:** Record every episode of *America's Funniest Videos*. End each day with a one-minute (one minute only) showing of those famous montages of silly people doing silly things. The students can't wait to come to your class to see what you have for them today.

7. **Catch them at their best:** Go see your students in a school play, music production, or athletic event. There is something emotional about seeing your kids in these passionate arenas.

8. **Dress the part:** If you look good, you feel good. It takes confidence to get up in front of an audience every day. I want you to stand in front of them with a swagger and bounce that exudes confidence. Change up your wardrobe and watch the audience focus on the "Star."

53

TEACHERS MAKE THE DIFFERENCE

I have come to the frightening conclusion that I am the decisive element in the classroom. It is my personal approach that creates the climate. It is my daily mood that makes the weather. As a teacher, I possess tremendous power to make a child's life miserable or joyous. I can be a tool of torture or an instrument of inspiration. I can humiliate or humor, hurt or heal. In all situations, it is my response that decides whether a crisis will be escalated or de-escalated and a child humanized or dehumanized.

—Dr. Hiam Ginott

NOTED CHILD PSYCHOLOGIST, Dr. Hiam Ginott, opened his book entitled *Teacher and Child* with the above quote. Ginott captures the essence of the power of teaching. To me, the most insightful and reflective portion of his comments come from the phrase, "In all situations, it is my response that decides." It is imperative that we remember that we are the adults and no matter how frustrated we get, we must conduct ourselves as professionals. We have a responsibility to use our power in a way that uplifts our children and never tears them down. There is an old saying that states: "Sticks and stones may break my bones, but words can never hurt me." Liar, liar, pants on fire. Words do hurt. They can cause tremendous damage to the best of us, furthermore, a developing child.

Please be cognizant of your power. In many cases, we spend more time with our students than their parents do. By being a consistent, caring adult presence, we can counteract the many negative forces today's kids face. Leo Buscaglia stated, "Too often we underestimate the power of a touch, a smile, a kind word, a listening ear, an honest compliment, or the smallest act of caring, all of which have the potential to turn a life around." His words should be a part of our daily reflection.

Thanks for loving our children!

54

DON'T JUST SURVIVE

*"There are countless ways of achieving greatness, but
any road to achieving one's maximum potential must be
built on a bedrock of respect for the individual, a commitment to excellence, and a rejection of mediocrity."*

—BUCK RODGERS

AS WE WRAP up this reflective guide to the wonderful world
of teaching, I want to thank you once again for being a
"teacher." It is the noblest of professions and requires
a missionary zeal that can truly exhaust the best of us.
There are going to be periods where survival is the best
you can do. However, if you are not careful, surviving will
be all you do for the rest of your career.

There is a significant difference between a twenty-year
teacher and a teacher who has been doing the same thing
for twenty years. The twenty-year teacher who continues
to grow and learn is one of the most prized possessions
we have. He or she has a wealth of knowledge and experience that you cannot put a price on. The teacher who has
been doing the same thing for twenty years is basically
a new teacher who has chosen not to grow and in turn
slowly dies.

I challenge you to keep growing and striving for excellence. Never doubt that you are a difference maker!
Whether they will admit it or not, the kids really do need

you. Your positive spirit can help them navigate the dangerous waters of childhood and adolescence.

If you find yourself currently in survival mode, it's okay. Like a distance runner who grabs water along the race, your educational journey requires time for refreshment. Don't be scared to reach for the water. You deserve to not just finish the race, but to cross the finish line with your hands held high. The key is to start *today*!

Good Luck and God Bless!

Lagniappe

"LAGNIAPPE" IS A French Creole word that is used in South Louisiana and Mississippi to mean "A little something extra." I still have all these rambling thoughts about education and life, so I decided to add the following reflections to compliment our time together.

Mr. Holland's Opus

IF YOU ARE an educator and have not seen this movie then you are required to rent it tonight and curl up on the couch for one of the best movies ever made. Richard Dreyfuss was nominated for an Academy Award for Best Actor in this 1995 movie that chronicles the life of a teacher and the trials and tribulations we all face. His four-decade journey is an inspiration for all teachers.

If you have already seen the movie, then you are required to see it once every year to remind yourself of the beauty of being a teacher.

SCHOOL SECRETARIES

WHAT CAN YOU say about these people who "truly run the school?" I have been blessed to be associated with several great school secretaries. Just like it is difficult to explain what we really do every day, it is equally impossible to give justice to the many hats a school secretary has to wear.

Whether it is putting a band-aid on a child, fixing the copier, giving out medicine, handling an irate parent, or using the intercom to tell everybody which bus is going to be late, the school secretary is vital to a school's success. A good one can save you, and a bad one will kill you.

Have you ever seen one of their paychecks? It is embarrassing. These difference-making people deserve our utmost respect. I know they can sometimes be cranky. However, see what happens if they don't come to work one day. Give some love to your secretaries. They deserve it.

SET THEM UP FOR SUCCESS

MANY OF YOUR students have never had academic success in school. Smart teachers will go out of their way to make sure students have success in those first few weeks. Most students will give you a good effort on those first assignments. Grade them and let them see a 100 or 92 on the top of the paper. This early feeling of achievement, along with a healthy dose of you bragging on them, might be just what they need to soar to new heights.

Thanks for doing the little extra things that set students up for success!

STRESS RELEASE

IF YOU ARE going to survive this crazy business called "teaching" you better find a healthy way to reduce stress. I have mentioned earlier that exercising is vital to becoming the best you can be. It is not selfish to set aside time for yourself. You cannot help others if you do not feel good yourself.

Another great way to reduce stress has nothing to do with excercise. This method is simple and does not cost a dime. Get in your car by yourself, put on your favorite CD, and turn it up as loud as you can. Sing your little heart out. There is something about singing and jamming in your car that makes all your troubles go away. Who cares if the guy next to you thinks you are crazy? You're a teacher; everyone knows you must be crazy.

TOP TEN REASONS TO BE A TEACHER

With apologies to David Letterman, here we go.

#10   Give a pop quiz whenever you want

#9   The joy of cafeteria food for life

#8   Constant exposure increases immunity from disease

#7   Never have to eat alone

#6   Stay Young – Pep rallies, Show and Tell

#5   Christmas and Spring Break

#4   June, July and August

#3   Fresh start every year (never boring)

#2   Insurance and Retirement

#1   Opportunity to Make a Difference

IF I WERE KING FOR THE DAY

1. **No school in my kingdom would be allowed to start classes before 8:30 am.** Well-rested teachers and kids make for happier campers.

2. **All parents would be required to substitute teach for one week.** Can you say teacher appreciation?

3. **All members of the school board and state legislature would be required to substitute for one week.** Can you say teacher pay raise?

4. **All principals would be required to teach a class for a week.** Can you say remember what it was like to be a teacher?

5. **All bus drivers, secretaries, janitors and cafeteria staff would be paid an appropriate salary.** Can you say what would we do without them?

6. **Every school in the kingdom would have a full-time nurse, counselor, and technology person on campus.** Can you say required if you want a well-run school?

7. **Every person in the kingdom would be required to enjoy a minimum of three workouts a week.** Can you say eat whatever you want?

8. **Prayer and the Pledge of Allegiance would be said at the start of every school day.** Can you say thankful for what we have?

9. **Every child would have two loving parents and a teacher who cared.** Can you say perfect world?

SOME THINGS HAVE CHANGED, SOME HAVE NOT

1872 Rules For Teachers (author unknown)

1. Teachers each day will fill lamps, clean chimneys.

2. Each teacher will bring a bucket of water and a scuttle of coal for the day's session

3. Men teachers may take one evening each week for courting purposes, or two evenings a week if they go to church regularly.

4. After ten hours in school, the teachers may spend the remaining time reading the Bible or other good books.

5. Women teachers who marry or engage in unseemly conduct will be dismissed.

6. Every teacher should lay aside from each days pay a goodly sum of his earnings for his benefit during his declining years so that he will not become a burden on society.

7. Any teacher who smokes, uses liquor in any form, frequents pool or public halls, or gets shaved in a barber shop will give good reason to suspect his worth, intention, integrity and honesty.

8. The teacher who performs his labour faithfully and without fault for five years will be given an increase of twenty-five cents per week in his pay, providing the Board of Education approves.

It is good to see that at least the pay increases have not changed very much over the years. I better cancel my appointment for a shave at the barber shop.

GREATNESS REQUIRES PERSISTENCE

The life of Abraham Lincoln serves as a role model for all educators.

Failed in business	1831
Defeated for legislature	1832
Failed in business again	1833
Elected to legislature	1834
Sweetheart died	1835
Had nervous breakdown	1836
Defeated for speaker	1838
Defeated for elector	1840
Defeated for congressional nomination	1843
Elected to Congress	1846
Defeated for Congress	1848
Defeated for Senate	1855
Defeated for Vice-President	1856
Defeated for Senate	1859
Elected President of the United States	1860

FAVORITE QUOTES

Success is not the key to happiness. Happiness is the key to success. If you love what you are doing, you will be successful.

—ALBERT SCHWEITZER

It is easy to be brave from a safe distance.

—AESOP

Education is what survives when what has been learned has been forgotten.

—B. F. SKINNER

The weak can never forgive. Forgiveness is the attribute of the strong.

—MOHANDAS K. GANDHI

Goodness is the only investment that never fails.

—HENRY DAVID THOREAU

Integrity without knowledge is weak and useless, and knowledge without integrity is dangerous and dreadful.

—SAMUEL JOHNSON

The purpose of human life is to serve and show compassion and the will to help others.

—ALBERT SCHWEITZER

Kind words can be short and easy to speak, but their echoes are truly endless.

—MOTHER TERESA

Opportunities are usually disguised as hard work, so most people don't recognize them.

—ANN LANDERS

Never lose sight of the fact that the most important yardstick of your success will be how you treat other people – your family, friends, and coworkers, and even strangers you meet along the way.

—BARBARA BUSH

The highest result of education is tolerance.

—HELEN KELLER

NOTES

1. Jim Collins, *Good to Great* (New York: Harper Collins, 2001).

2. Harry Wong and Rosemary Wong, *The First Days of School* (Mountain View, CA: Harry Wong Publications, 1998).

3. John Maxwell, *The 21 Indispensable Qualities of a Leader* (Nashville, TN: Thomas Nelson Publisher, 1999).

4. Rick Pitino, *Success is a Choice* (New York: Broadway Books, 1997).

5. Carol Ann Tomlinson, *The Differentiated Classroom: Responding to the needs of all learners* (Alexandria, VA: Association for Supervision and Curriculum Development, 1999).

6. Hiam Ginott, *Teacher and Child* (New York: McMillan, 1972).

7. James Dobson, *Focus on the Family* (Colorado Springs, Colorado, 1996).

8. Kyla Wahlstrom, "Changing Times: Findings from the First Longitudinal Study of Later High School Start Times" (*NASSP Bulletin*, December 2002).

9. National Training Laboratories (Bethel, Maine).

10. William Glasser, "Ten Steps to Good Discipline" (*Today's Education*, Nov.–Dec. 1977).

Quotations not specifically noted were found on the following Web sites:

www.quoteland.com
www.quotationspage.com

"COMMON SENSE" STAFF DEVELOPMENT

DR. BENIGNO HAS spoken extensively on the keys to classroom management and the role teachers play in making a difference in the lives of young people. Using music, video clips, and real-world examples, his high-energy presentations have informed and entertained thousands of teachers.

For more information on programs presented by Dr. Chuck Benigno, please go to www.ExcellenceorSurvival.com.

Presentations:

- Teaching: Excellence or Survival?
- Principalship: Excellence or Survival?
- Life: Excellence or Survival? (Student Audience)
- Teachers Make the Difference
- Counselors Make the Difference
- Preparing Students for the 21st Century Workforce
- New Teacher Induction Program

Contact Dr. Chuck Benigno:
chuckbenigno@aol.com